Awakening Poems
Enlightenment at Your Fingertips

Suba

Copyright © 2015 Tobias Moore (Suba)

All rights reserved.

ISBN-10: 0985167254
ISBN-13: 978-0985167257

CONTENT

My Other Writings	4
Process Poetry	5
Journey's Beginning	7
Obstacles	17
Practices	59
Self-Conscious-Energy	113
Being Fully Present and Enjoying	139
Enlightenment	153
Characteristics, Qualities, & Signs	169
Meditations on Ramana's 40 Verses	199
Random	209
About Author	239

MY WRITINGS

Process Poetry Series

Words to a Friend
Money Poems: Piecing 2-Gether Wealth, Health, Happiness, and Wisdom
Sacred Herb Poems
Awakening Poems: Enlightenment at Your Fingertips

Guides

A Guide for the Homeless: Skills for Surviving the Streets
A Guide for Crisis Responders: Skills for Crisis Interventions

Other

A Different Road: From Bum to Mystic (*my traveling memoires*)
Arbatel Workings: Meditations and Rituals
Path of Christ: Awakening Compassion Within

PROCESS POETRY

Process Poetry is my way of coming to know something. I ask questions and then put myself in a receptive state to receive the answers. Through that process I receive insights into the nature of my inquiry. Everything becomes very clear.

The poems and pithy sayings in this collection arose from years of study, meditation, ritual, introspection, practice, and cultivation.

To benefit from my words I suggest you meditate on them. Allow the words to sink into your being and open you to new ways of seeing and relating with yourself and the world around you.

I encourage you to write in this book. Take notes next to each poem or pithy saying: scratch out things you don't agree with, fill in areas that need more information, color these pages with your thoughts, ideas, insights, understandings, experiences, practices, and so on. This is your book and your life.

These are my questions
answers
practices
understandings
experiences.

This is my process,
My way

JOURNEY'S BEGINNING

What Triggers the Journey?
Sometimes it's Sickness
　　　　Loss
　　　　Pain
　　　　Trauma
　　　　Death,

Other times it's Fear & Uncertainty
Or A Desire for more,
Curiosity, Intense Experiences,

Identity crisis, A Moment of Clarity,

　　Drugs, Questioning, Tranquility,

Need for acceptance, wholeness,
Hunger for power & control,
Wanting order & understanding,
　　　　and on and on...

What stone,
what pebble stubs our toe,

shifting,
but for a second,
the direction we go?

Reprieve,
for even a moment,
lets us see what's there.

Sometimes we just fall into it
while serving ourselves.

You never know
what will wake you up,

So be open to it all...

Healing truly is a blessing...

Aging
Sickness
Trauma
Death

Pain

Should we wallow in it?
No.
Fixate?
No.
Elevate? Spiritualize? Energize?
No.

It's just pain.

Be with it.
Take care of yourself.
Nuture and love your body & Mind.
Have compassion.

No matter how you play it,
      Pain Hurts

Just one obstacle is enough
to begin practicing,
One supporting virtue/quality
to get things moving,
One positive thought
to get started,
One action to make it happen.

As Laotzu says,
"A journey of a thousand miles
starts with a single step,"
Before you know it,
          You've Arrived

The hardest part
is knowing the Question —
that's what the journey
is all About.

And what is this Question?

Who am 👁️ ?

OBSTACLES

What Resists?

Stupidity
Ignorance
Conceptualization
Fear
Doubt
Desire
Anger
Attachment
Dishonesty
Selfishness
Sloth
Procrastination
Boredom
Aimless
Lack of focus
Restless
Agitation

Cloudiness
Sickness
Unbalancing
   Environments
   Relations
   Thoughts
   Emotions
   Beliefs
Excessiveness
Distractions
Anxiety
etc...

It's easy to not practice,
to be tired
    distracted
    drained
    depressed
    agitated
    muddled
    doubtful.

It takes strength & courage,
a strong desire
indomitable will
patience & fortitude
constant Awareness
    diligence
    & vigilance to walk a Path.

It ONLY takes a small crack to Sink a Ship

Shortcuts
do
sometimes
get
us
there
quicker,
other times they make things harder

Things keep bubbling up.
There's still murkiness agitation.
What's up with that?

you're still waiting to reach a goal

    finish a book
    meet the right person
    find the right tools –
        the right moment
    Let go of the last layer
    Learn the ultimate truth
    Experience the really real

Is it crazy
to keep running after the finish line?
to keep reading
       studying
         reaching
for other avenues to Enlightenment
when we've already found it?

is it fear
    desire
  or attachment
        getting in the
              Way?

- [x]
- [x]
- [x]
- [x]
- [x]
- [x]
- [x]
- [x]
- [x]
- [ ]
- [ ]
- [ ]
- [ ]
- [ ]

There's always More...

Stop preparing for The Day

and live it

There's nothing that ruins the moment more than thinking of some other time'.

---
1. Past or Future

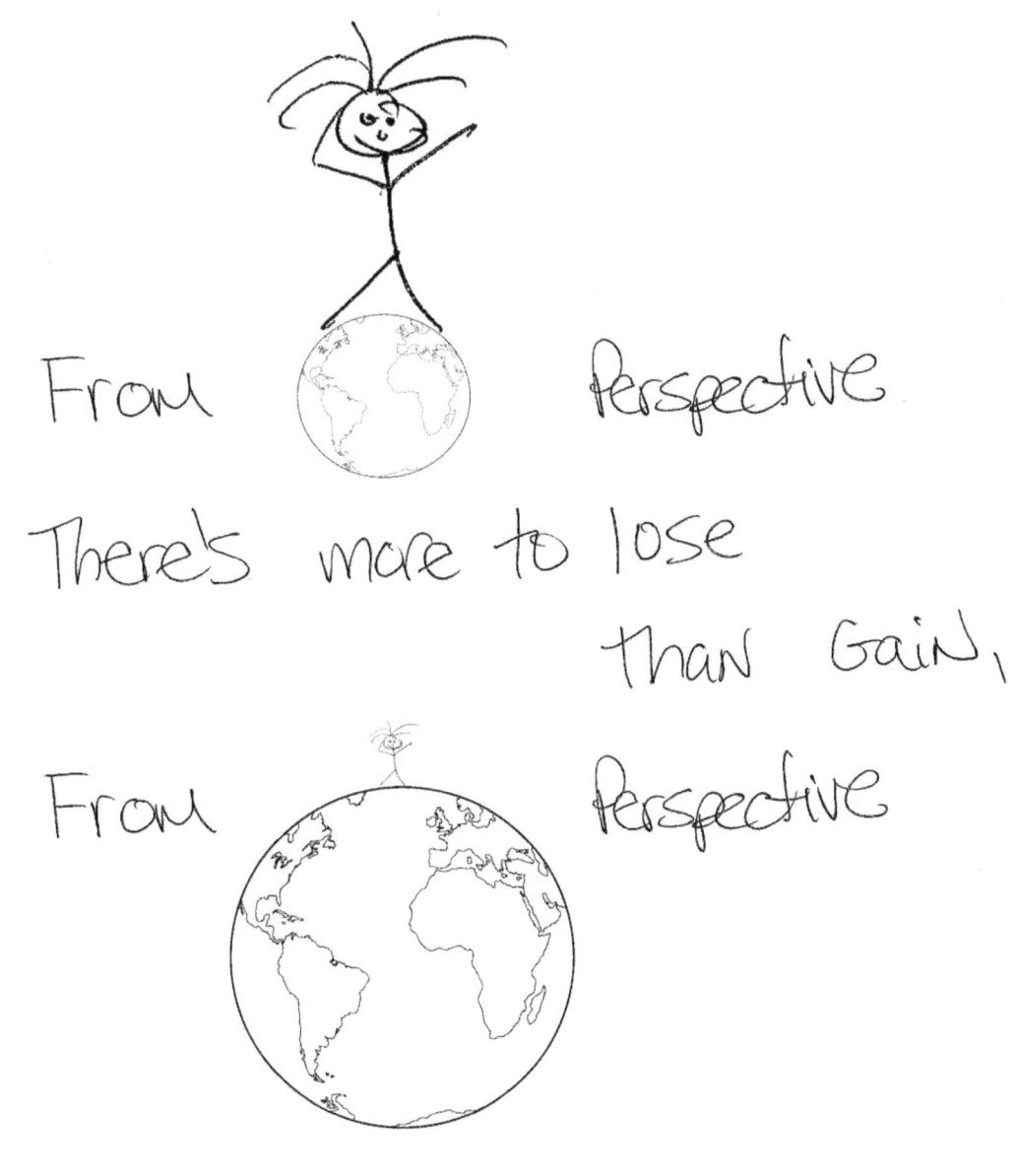

From 🌍 Perspective
There's more to lose
than Gain,
From 🌍 Perspective
There's more to Gain

Distractions
both mentally & physically
are ripples within the mind

Everything pales
to the worry of making
　　　　　Ends Meet/Meat

That's what occupies
the lion's share of the Mind.

I fear change
       pain
         loss

I fear losing my mind
              Body
                Self

I'm afraid of living
         and dying

I'm afraid of murderous nuns
and conniving babies

I'm afraid of the self
       and what it's capable of.

One of my greatest fears is that I will not come back after Awakening.

Is that because

    A. Altruism
    B. Afraid and Attached

Circle Your Answer

The fear
that science, religion, society &
family will be forgotten
lost
neglected
rejected is silly.

Enlightenment does not create darkness, ignorance, seperation or denial, it illuminates the connections & wholeness of All.

Desire will lie
cheat
steal
murder:

Did you not exist
before its arrival —
Was/Is life so miserable
without it?

Craving is like
reaching for the next chip
even before
we've finished the current one.

Being full is when <u>we stop</u>
Reaching
consuming.
That's what <u>we do</u> to be

Fulfilled as well...

what makes this moment any different than the moment right before you got what you desired?

The Mind

What enrages me?

waiting
failed expectations
lack of control
Insults to my identity
 and its extensions

Being hurt
neglected
Abused

Not being heard
or understood

being judged
being rejected

Having to let go...

I'm jealous,
being poor sucks,
being unhealthy sucks.

Leakage

Sadness
Depression
Hopelessness
Empty
Heavy

    What's the point
    Who cares
    Nothing matters
      No one understands...

Darkness — All Alone — <u>USELESS</u>.

👁 see you Pride

Planting yourself in the mind
like a weed in fertile soil.

Catching you while still young
I pull you out and lay you
on the ground to wither and die
before the sun's awareness.

What's this doubt?

That Enlightenment exists?

No

That there are practices that invite it?

No

That there's Awake People?

No

That you can do it?

Residual   Energy
Patterns
Aspects
Characteristics
Behaviors
Beliefs ...

It's possible,
Some have Awoken.
And being that
we're all one:
we're all awake.

I Love Fallacizing

I have this ideal image
of myself:
    Awake
    Enlightened
    Illuminated

The most subtle and beautiful
obstacle of them all...

Like taunt cobwebs
 flickering in the sun,
We see our attachments
when death comes knocking

What thoughts?
 Regrets?
What memories arise?
What dreams?
What names and faces —
 what disgraces?
What desires / inclinations?
What pulls you back?

what am i attached to?

Body
self
concepts
beliefs
identity
relationships
control
desires
possessions
dreams
life

. . .

The tighter the fist holds on

The harder it is to receive.

There's a lot of hang-ups:

How it's supposed to B
what conditions R Right
what needs to B Done
when will it Happen

where

why.
    There's just the Here & Now,
        it's really that simple

The soul is
the ego's greatest
　　most cherished
　　　highest expression
　　　　　of self :

A most subtle Attachment

when you are not ready,
        you're knot Ready.

when you are,
        U R.

why get tied up about it?

I'm afraid

You say,
"i don't deserve it."

It's not a deserving issue,
there's just somethings
the 👁 cannot see

i don't
i can't
i won't
i know

I will :

and so we sow...

So how was the mind today?

Tired   HEAVY

Contemplative   LUSTFULL

Frustrated   Agitated   Anxious   Studious

Angry   Thoughtful

Greedy   Selfish

Remembering   Quiet

Deceitful   Loving   Receptive

Uncomfortable

Hopeful   Impatient   Ungrounded   OPEN   Fantasizing

Kind

Seperation Between

This & That
Sacred & Mundane
Emptiness / Fullness
Conscious / Unconscious

Self / ?

When these disappear,
what's left,
    just I<u>s</u>

Why do we hold enlightenment hostage?

Trying to negotiate
 bribe
 blackmail
 ransom it into Being

as if its something we trade for:

 I'll do this
 let this go
 et cetera...

The hard part of the Path is not knowing what to do, but the actual doing it.

I've studied under duress
while stifled
   & overworked.
I've meditated and done ritual
while poor & in debt;
harrassed by ravenous wolves
collecting their share of meat.
I've practiced in the rain
    covered in snow
wrapped in three torn blankets -
    teeth chattering.
In the darkness of darkness
   i still reach for the light;
  There's no excuse
     to not Practice.

PRACTICES

My Path

Honest Inquiry
Clear Seeing
Genuine Intention
Cultivation
Embodying
Empowerment
Enjoying
Sharing

Believe in the Possibilities.

Believe in yourself.

We'll never hit the target as long as we're still holding The Arrow

If we truly wanted something,

why would we not Move towards it?

A criminal would rarely commit
a crime
if
at some level
they did not trust in the possibility
of Reward & Escape.

Why would we ever choose to
practice if we did not
at some level
believe in the Awakened state,
that there are things we can do to achieve it,
and that people have & are doing it.

Trust

any root word with "us" in it
should be given attention,

for they us<u>a</u>lly imply a
relationship between All of US

All those qualities you imagine
Enlightenment to Be,
those are the practices you
work with.

And if
by chance
these qualities are not quite there,
@ <
they invite more light into
the world through Us

Some Helpful Things

Act
Be Curious
Question
Focus
Listen
Possitivity
Honesty
Intentional
Open
Be Present
Aware
Simplicity
Humble
Non-reactive
Preemptive

Trusting
Content
Loving
Compassionant
Joyful
Studious
Fasting
Chanting
Prayer
Recollecting
Cultivative
Meditative
Stillness
Quietude

while letting go }

Judgment
Jealousy
Regret
Fear
Attachment
Doubt

It's easy to overlook,
to forget the doing
when we're so caught up
reaching to learn and
comprehend.

Without the experience of doing
there's no true understanding.

Some Beneficial Conditions

Ability
Capacity
Aptitude
Desire
Will
Fortitude
Practical Knowledge
Understanding
Honesty
. . .

what imbalances you?

How/where/when did it Arise?
what's it constituded of – formed by?
what triggers? why?
what grows it?
what weakens it?
what thoughts dissolve it?

Recognize all the opportunity to

Practice

When you're caught up mentally
emotionally
physically
energetically
...

That's the moment,

This is where the action is -
where the work begins ...

Don't worry about what they're thinking, just take control of your own.

Take the <u>time</u>
create the <u>space</u>
invite the <u>energy</u>,
embrace <u>matter</u>

These are the <u>building blocks</u>

    4 consciousness
    2 experience
    1 - ness

Become Aware

When we know the target or @ least its Direction, we're better able to Hit ⟶ ⊙(it)

Practice

Start with what is,
If the body is sick,
allow it to heal;
If the mind is twisted,
relax and allow it to unwind.

There's no need to hide
There's no where to run
There's no where to go

Just be present

There's Just Now : Right Now

It's okay to hurt,
be in pain,

it's when we cover it up,
    hide from it,
    run away,
    justify it,

That's when we suffer.

Don't ignore[1] it,
whatever "it" may Be.

Shine light[2] upon it,

That's The Way,

U C[3]

---
1. ignorance
2. Awareness
3. You See

Deal with imbalances as they arise:
No procrastinating

If you see an unbalancing thought or action, apply its Remedy Right Away

It's easier to remove a weed before it takes root

Cleaning a mess as it happens is the surest way to avoid clutter

---

Fixing a problem when its small is the best way to prevent an issue from arising

---

Know the triggers, signs & behaviors, symptoms, feeling, thoughts & consequences of unwanted states of mind and sever them before they manifest in your life.

One-pointedness leads to Samadhi:

The easiest way to achieve Samadhi is to find something you like and focus on it's sensations
images
concepts
sounds
tastes
etc...

Once you've found your perfered focus, use it as an anchor to stabalize your mind.

Now,
  immerse
    yourself
      in the experience

Focus on the possitive qualities and the unhealthy ones will fall away on their own.

Letting go
Slowing down
Opening
Softening
Breathing
Touching into the moment
Being fully Present & Aware

all seem to light up the moment.

My Question is,
 "How do we sustain it?"

Practice
Practice
Practice
 'til it becomes Natural

Anger
Jealousy } Don't Feed

Regret
Fear } Confront Directly

Doubt } Let go

Trust
Contentment
Love and compassion
Joyfulness

Stop role-playing,
what-ifs.

Stop looking back,
regreting.

Stop day dreaming,
fantasizing.

Don't get lost in the Head.

You have to be okay
to let come,
    come,
& then
    Let it Go.

No matter the diabolical/
debaucherous thought
or Greatest Insight,
You have to be okay
to let it Go......

Keep knocking
Keep conditioning
Keep telling yourself what you want

        Inflame the passions
        Warm the Heart
        Clarify the Mind
        Drive the body

Raise the Vibration
Burn away all obstacles
        all illusions

C TIME
    For what it Is

Just do what
U R
doing

How the fuck do we let go of expectations?

The very act of letting go implies
that we expect them to go:
   Somethings fishy About that

The very movement towards enlightenment
naturally lightens things up:
  less baggage
  AND brighter

Don't try to change everything at once

Start with 1 thing
give your focus & energy to it
invite it in
embody it

Then move on to the next.

Don't rush — for everything has the potential to wake you up

And

Don't worry so much about getting rid of things — they leave on their own

Honesty

Be Patient,

It takes time to Grow

Both love & compassion open us to the moment & all that's within it.

NO MINDLESSNESS

Cultivate willpower and take control of your life.

How to be content?

Start by recognizing the blessings in life, then pay attention to what invites those blessings and what does not. Cultivate those qualities, actions, & thoughts that invite contentment.

Joyfulness

A practice of lightening up a space, inviting possitivity, happiness, openess, and Blessedness.

It's like the sun peaking through the clouds on a wet, cold, dark, and miserable day.

Joy is a ray of light
full of warmth

Having no idea is
a great place
to start

Why am I giving up this moment for some future one?

Invite the mind's curiosity:

   What does it feel like?
   What's its perspective?
      Likes - dislikes?
  What's it made of?

Keep asking <u>questions</u>!
for as the mind searches for answers
it comes closer & closer to the
object of its focus.
Leading us inevitably
      to make contact
and get to know it directly:

                    Samadhi
―――――――――
" Quest - I - ON

As long as the mind clings
to insight,
there's attachment:

"A Golden chain, is still a chain,"
I heard someone say once.

The mind must relinquish to the moment of experience in order to Transcend Itself

Getting out of the Head and into the body is a great place to start.

As the inner gate opens
a deep reservoir stirs,
rippling into our daily lives.

Listen
follow the voice

Embody its wisdom

Look @ the doubt:
where does it spring from?

B

M(fully in the)OMENT

It's not always easy,
you wouldn't have to
practice if it was :)

SELF-CONSCIOUS-ENERGY

The more Energy
The faster the vibration:

A Particle of Being (SAT)
A Ray of Light (CHIT)
A Wave of Delight (ANANDA)

Dissolving Self in Other:
It's not
hate me, love them,
belittling self for others,
wishing them well-being
    while harboring their pain.

If there's no difference between
    self & other,

Then hating this drop is no better
than hating that drop:
    both poison the ocean...

Meditating on the grotesque
Pushes away,
Meditating on the beautiful
Opens things up,
Both dissolves the ego's boundries:
One strips away everything
The other loses itself to All.

What happens to "The Self?"
Which self?

The Empty 1
or The Whole One

One loses its identity through perpetual change, the other through oneness.

Either way,
That's the end of its story.

Becoming smaller,
what was solid
    is now insubstantial.

Becoming bigger,
what was solid
    is now insignificant.

Let go of self,
see the interconnection,
experience the spaciousness.

Is there a self?
What is a self?

Where does it come from – originate?
Why? For what purpose?
Is it a composition or singularity?
Created or Eternal?
Does it develop or is it unchanging?
Layered or simple?
A conceptual model or a thing?
Epiphenominal or GOD?
A Given or something stolen?
A rain drop or the ocean itself?
A Beholder / Partaker / Enjoyer?
A lens of consciousness?
A subject or object
A point or wave

Who is this speaking?
Who's Listening?
Questioning?
Answering?

Who is this?
Who are you?

I AM WE R ⊙

what am i?
That shifty thing,
the more 👁 look
the less 👁 see,
down, down,
the rabbit hole,
That crazy journey of the Soul:

Three clicks

I'M HOME

when consciousness

emBodies mINd

I see no permanent self,
just a composit of particles
all subsumed under this identity—
 this self.

Take enough away,
damage enough cells,
 and that self disappears,

Replaced by another.

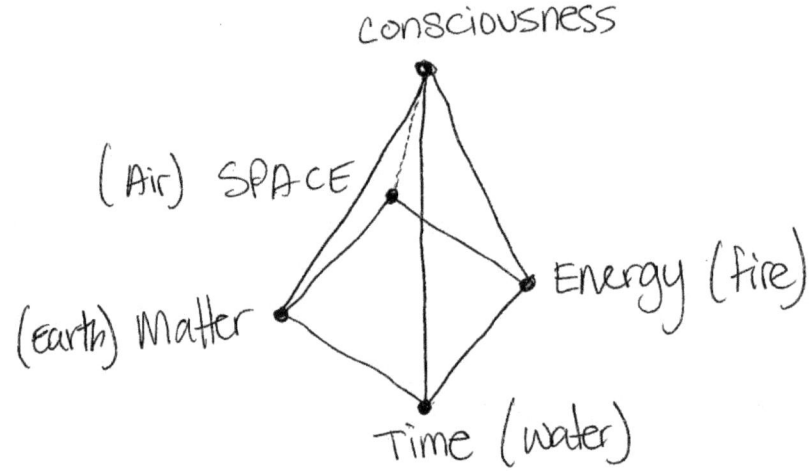

Elements of Life

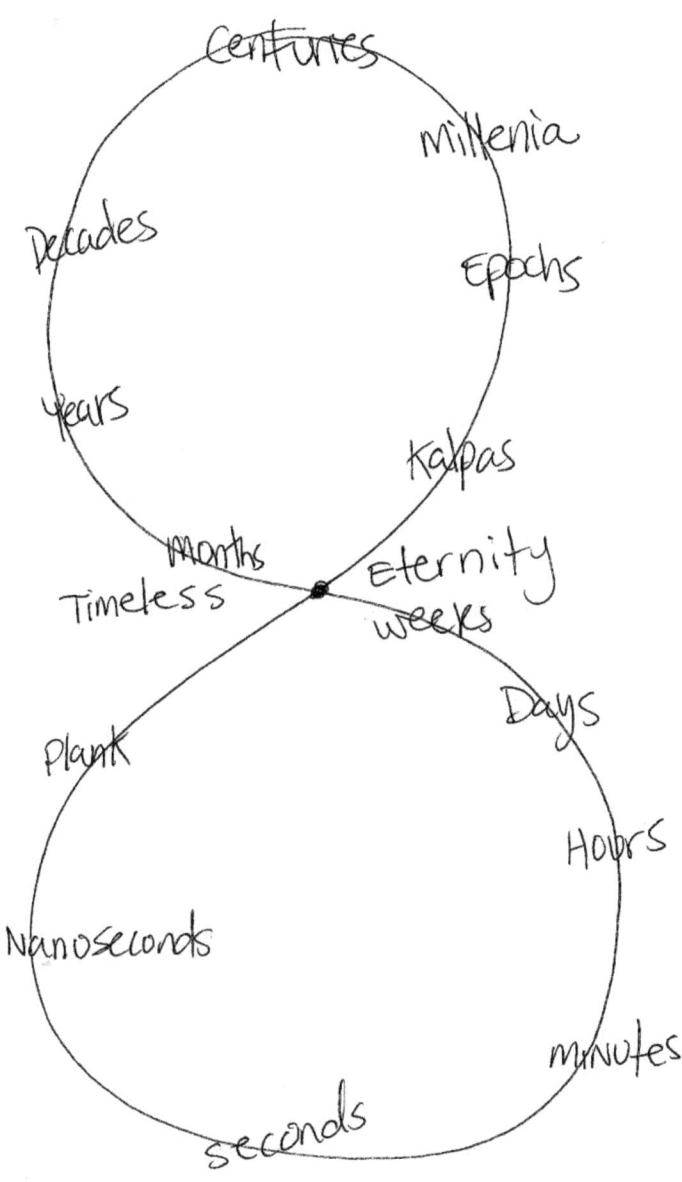

A moment in time...

Being present
is much like the
speed of light

time slows
movement becomes still
space opens up
Everything's Clear

Shifting particles
Binding together
Transmuting
 and moving on.

At the rudimentary level
even particles lack a core identity:

changing spin
        speed
        charge
        ...

        where is its' self?

from particles arise atoms
                      molecules
                      proteins
                      organs

and on up the chain of complexity.

when does the core self arise?

The first sign of consciousness
is an elemental particle's
preference to attract or repulse:
to connect or not connect.

Particles of Self

I'm the unfolding karma
of an unimaginable #
of Beings
Living out this moment,
Right here and Now,
collectively,
as this self called Tobias

There are particles within us that
are Awake,
that had
@ some point in time & space
been asleep
and then became part of an
Awakened Body/Mind.
Now They Blissfully float Around
Awakening whatever They touch.
We need only identify with
those particles of our being
and Grow them into who we R

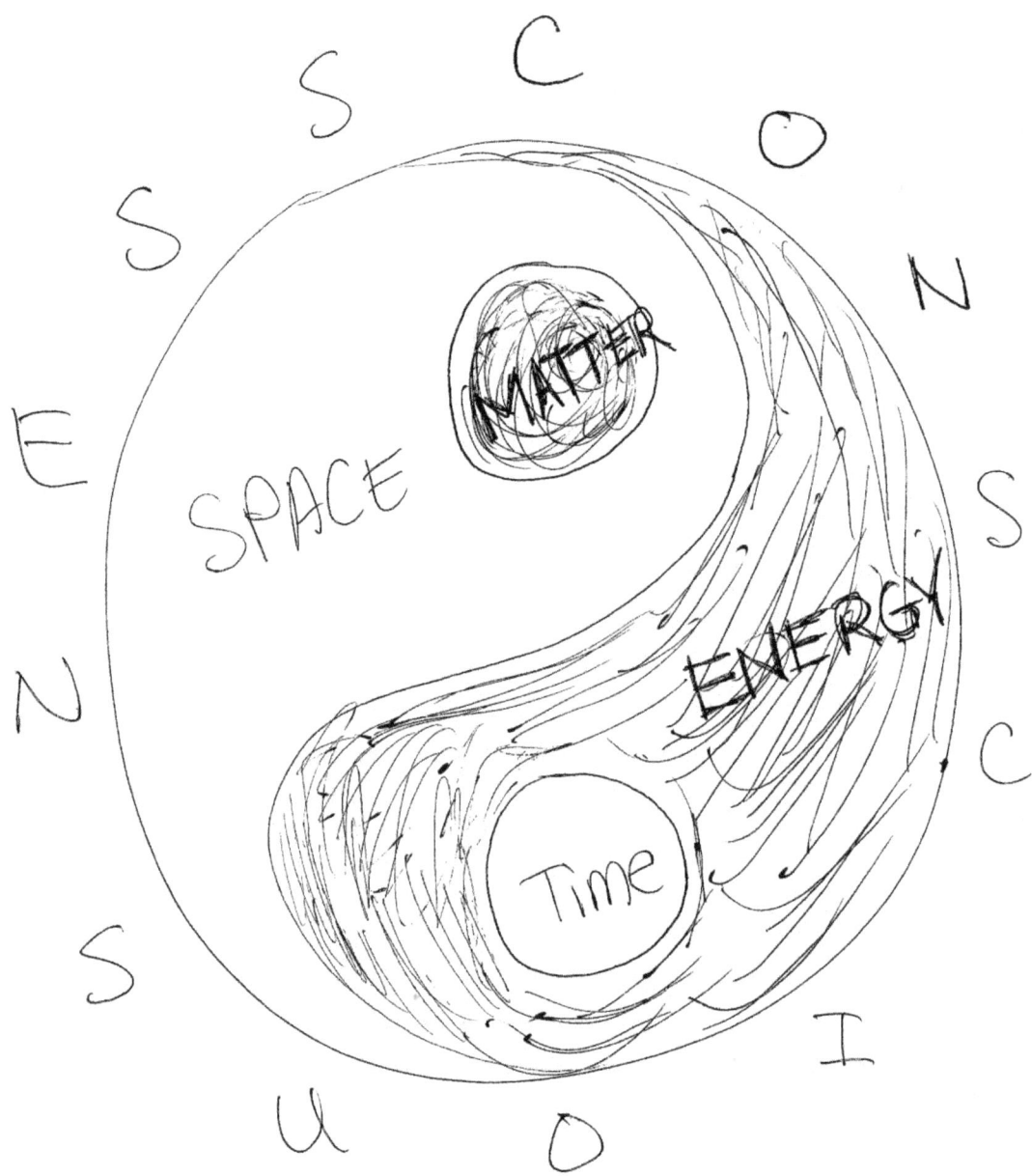

There's a flow to energy, learning how to tap into it is key.

Tap in
Direct
Become the flow.

That's Dao

There's power in the moment: an unfiltered, unlimited source of energy just waiting to B tapped into.

without preperation & Direction
inviting more energy into
an unfit container/channel
only exsaperates Problems.

There's a direct connection
between energy & our state of mind.

The more present the mind
The more energy there is.

When the mind is restless/agitated
energy drains away   occupied
                            obsessed

When the mind craves
              clings
              hungers
energy is consumed

When the mind is clouded
                 unfocused
                 confused

energy is stagnant

What's the connection between energy & enlightenment

The more energy,
the brighter things get;
just be careful
not to burn out.

Gradually increase the energy
while purifying & conditioning
the pathways of body & mind.

Then channel it to one thing
and the light
　　　　you'll find...

Why does energy help?

Beyond the fact that energy intensifies our experiences, inviting deeper & more encompassing states of Being.

It strengthens us, giving us energy to do with as we will

PRESENT

Awareness = conscious attention

Just drop the baggage and enjoy.

Feel
smell
taste
hear
see
perceive
think

touching in — Samadhi

People are in such a hurry
desperately rushing
running
hiding
reaching
grasping
clinging

Relax
SLOW DOWN

ENjoy
B IN-joy

Stopping,
we look through,
it's the same on both sides.

There's a curiosity though,
a wonder,
There's something to be seen.

like trying to look through
the slats of a fence while
driving by...

At some point we have
to stop writing
acting
doing
thinking

And just experience

Stop thinking about the next moment and just be present with what is.

Keep Reminding Yourself

Be Here Now

Breathe

Enjoy

There's no Deep [Secret] ELEVATED
thing to know –
experience.

There's just NOW
Right HERE
   in this place
        space
          and time,
   So ENjoy

There's no better way to
invite more time & space
than 2 B

Fully Present & Aware:

To Focus on What Is....

conscious
  slow eating:
Grape in mouth
  slicing teeth
    juices flowing –
sweet nectar.

Crushing molars –
  alchemy unfolds.

Pay Attention
Be Aware

Witness its color & shape
Taste the subtleties
Feel the textures
Inhale the moment
Become it's essence

ENJOY

Life is the Greatest Gift
a child can tear into:
Let them enjoy
   the Present :)

Your life is happening

Right

NOW

ENLIGHTENMENT

I see it,
I hear
and understand,
and I'm beginning to wonder,

"am I awake?"

Want
strive
open
invite

more light[1] & lightness[2] into your life: where that leads, only time will tell...

---

1. Insight
2. Less attachments/weight; more joy, happiness, & compassion

Just because we're enlightened doesn't mean we can fly — we haven't wings.
Nor does it mean we can grow back legs or create something out of nothing.
Enlightenment just shines light on what is.

Will we be omniscient?
No.
Walk on water, Fly through the air?
No.

Don't let that stop you.

Is it Instant or Gradual?

To some
it's Instant,
for the rest of us,
            it's Gradual.

In truth though,
it's neither,
for what's time got to
do with it?

It's true,
Enlightenment is instantaneous;
it just happens
there's a lot of work/practice
to create the conditions
for it to Arise

Sometimes enlightenment comes
like the Rising Sun:
Slowly Brightening

Are there degrees of Enlightenment?

No,
that's just unenlighted perspective.

Is it Blissful all the time?

If bliss means being free from
    discomfort
    pain
    sickness
    and death,
      Then No.

If it means being fully Present, aware, and free of suffering,

    Then Yes

How does a drop of water express being part of the ocean?

More me?

Enlightenment is like winning
    the lottery,
The odds are against us,
and yet,
it happens every day

The Heavenly Mind
The Earthly Body

R ♡ 1

Enlightenment leaves a
Ripple
whose presence we recognize
in those qualities we seek
 to invite

flowing

NO RE=sistance:

A Stream within a Stream

CHARACTERISTICS
QUALITIES
SIGNS

Some Characteristics, Qualities & Signs

Kindness
Joyful
Content
Free
Humble
Tranquil / Peaceful
Honest
Connected
Simple
Fresh
Open
Spontaneous
Understanding
Unhindered
Patient
Wise

Disciplined
Certain
Unattached
Clear
Still
Authentic
Truthful
Blissful
Compassionant
Spacious
Focused
Aware
Fully Present
Accepting
Flexible
Friendly
Generous
Grateful
and so much more...

SOME SIGNS

Knowing
Flowing
Growing

There's a sense of knowing
    Themselves
    Others
    Reality

There's a sense of flowing
    Seemless movement
    Still
    Powerful
    Eternal
    Empty, yet whole

There's a sense of Growing,
for everything around them breathes
    Expands
    Widens
    Deepens
    Rises
    OPENS...

Compassion
Simplicity
Humbleness

That's what Lao-Tzu says

when you're tired of disappointing yourself

―――

when you're tired of being tired

―――

when what you believe & R are the same

If joy, happiness, contentment, freedom, peacefulness, connection, freshness, openness, understanding, wisdom, insight, patience, and so forth are entering into your life more,

then You're Headed in A Blessed Direction

You know you're on a path to enlightenment when you start noticing the connection between all things.

That Desire for MORE becomes Less and Lesssssss.....

There's No Need

There's no shame, Doubt or inhabition

Need and fear
    are no where
            to be found

The mind is very Quiet

certainty

Being fully present:
no desire to chase
or fear to run,
no attachment to hold onto
or obstacle to block our way,
no anger to burn
or jealousy to consume us.

Nothing but the bare moment
as it is.

No thought unseen

There's complete Transparency:
No Thing Hid
No Shadow
No Ripples

There's direct knowledge of self

crystal clear
fully Aware
Complete Focus
A spotless mirror
An unrippled pond
The Vaste & cloudless sky

Who R U?

Something
   hidden behind
           a thing?

Layers
Turtles
Links in an Ouroboros chain

Just 👁 & 👁

The Rasta Say: 👁

There's no tolerance for ignorance & negativity
Rather than listen to someone bitch & complain, they direct them to their joys, to what invites happiness
clarity
wisdom
connection
& so on...

Supporting & Freeing

The words flowing from their lips
fill our cups to overflowing:

Nurishing & healing
strengthening & encouraging

Rather than   Annoyance
              spite
              jealous
              or anger,
we find ourselves open, receptive,
aware, overwhelmed, joyful, and
at peace when we're around Them.

Humbleness

a soft refrain
a gentle touch
subtle movements

A deep Heart felt Exchange:

Breathing out

"HAAaaaa..."

There's a simple
certain
complete
Helpfulness

There's no need to do
                    say
                    or think

There's an experience
      of spaciousness,
where anything is possible.

There's a sense of coming into the moment: it's almost too easy.

There's a feeling of

Relaxing

INTO

The MOMENT

Magic Happens

How does our Relationship with the world & others change?

There's more clarity, Love
openness, Peace
Honesty, Joy
Integrity, Abundance
Patience, Connection
Understanding, Fluidity
Compassion, Ground
Wisdom & so forth

I'd imagine it would be a good relationship.

So to answer the question,

it would change for the Better.

A child removes rocks from
the stream:
The current becomes smooth.

No judgment or intention,
just playful innocence
open curiosity
and a delight in the moment
of Pure Being

MEDITATIONS ON RAMANA'S 40 VERSES

those murderous thoughts,
those loving thoughts;
there's no difference,
they're just thoughts floating by.

holding on,
attachment,
the i;
to form
and from form,
differences arise.

some likeable,
a few loveable,
most inconsequential
or outright undesirable.

I've experienced the mind as the Universe,
not as a thing within it,
but as a thing that encompasses it.

we use words like joy
connection
openness
passion
trust
god
unity
and family
to describe love,
but no matter how many words,
formulas,
or things we use to define it,
nothing can prepare us for what it's like to be in Love.

In the same way,
there are no words to describe Enlightenment.

there's ultimately no self,
for self is just another word we use to point with

Some say the Divine is the death of matter, as in, DIeVine,
others see it as Pure Embodied Consciousness, as in, DIVeIN$_E.$

we hold onto the Purusha,
the Soul,
that I/True Self,
Pure Witness,
because we're afraid to let go
of that last little pin holding us to-gether

I've Awoken,
now I just need to remain awake:
to bad Starbucks can't help with that☺

it's not a seeing and understanding,
but a knowing,
and we only truly know,
when we K<u>now</u>,
and that comes only in the Now:
right now
in this moment
am I…

We are reaching beyond the MiND,
that prison of the i,
that place where thoughts lie.

RANDOM

Sometimes it's not the message but the messanger that's important:

I remember being on my Big Wheeler
circling around and around
on the driveway.

Going up
I yearned for the moon
Going down
I was the moon

Timothy Leary reminded me of this
when I asked him what the
meaning of life is:

"Up & Down, Up & Down"
He told me...

The point of these meditations
is not to assume or possess

Enlightenment

But to learn about it
so as to Awaken

It's not just about reading and comprehending,

It's also about the Actions that bring it about.

It's better to fail
and keep trying
than to live a life full of Regret
and never knowing the possibilities.

The Heart is the center.

Reason without compassion is a scary place

You really fucked us
Descartes,
we're not just thoughts.

There's a difference between thinking of something and experiencing it.

To think¹
or not to think²?

That B A Question
       ⎵
Need at least this to understand it
and a PhD to have an answer

---

1. mucking up things
2. Mental diet

I lose the question
in the answer.

I have to retrace my steps
to understand.

Flickering images
slowing down:
      Stillness.

Speeding up,
one still moment into the next:
      Fluidity / continuity.

Everything you experience,
be it with body or mind,
has the seed of Samadhi
within it.

How could anything be boring?

THE First Mara,
    a hopeful future.

THE second,
    a utopian Past

THE LAST,
    a boreing and
        regretable Present.

I resist & gringe from pain while openly consuming and being consumed by desire.

My Anger destroys the peace and attachments rip me apart.

All these disappear through common sense and habit: A thing we <u>wear</u>

inside
A
N
D
OUT

It's easier sometimes to forgive & have compassion for an enemy than to do the same for family & self.

Warmth
Compression
Light massage
    Gentle touch
    Soft caress.

Slow
Smooth
Gentle movements:
        Spontaneous Qi Gong.

Soften
Breathe
Relax
        allow the energy to flow
                to grow.

Patience
Compassion
Openness
        Healing is an unveiling,
        a journey of self-discovery,
        a process of Awakening.

Trails are not just about arriving

They're also <u>Pathways</u> to
    understanding
    Pleasure
    Joyfulness
    Blissful Happiness

  Learning
  Growing
  Experiencing

                Insight
                Peace
                Wisdom

I saw my littlest looking out
into space
      Searching within her mind.
I almost pulled her back by saying
    "answer me"
    "what are you looking at"
    "You're spacing out"
    "Hello?"

Instead,
    I just watched in awe

It seems weird
to meditate on Enlightenment
as if
it's an object to subjectify.

why wouldn't we,
it's the best of subjects
and the object of my full Attention

Just because
the words spout from my mouth
doesn't mean I am the source

I'm just a spring in the ground
from which the water flows
       through

Seek the Flowing River,
Step from its shores:
No dirt rises
No ripples form.

Letting go
Flowing,
No-thing to disturb
    THE MIND

I like this voice,
this channel,
these thoughts.
I like the feeling
　　　of Growing,
　　　　　EXPANDING,
　　Deeper & more encompassing.
I understand what it means
　　　　　to open,
　　　　　to let go,
to allow the Spirit to flow through.
I only wish to remain here,
Bringing this state
　　　　　Everywhere 🌀 GO...

when two become one:

2 2 1 1

There's no light
    without darkness
No Death
    without life
No Awakening
    without sleep
No Enlightenment
    without Ignorance
No Witness
    without the Witnessed

No matter how clever the mind
you can never truly know
because you're stuck inside

The ego is the
event-horizon of the Self

Everything I know about the Dao is between these two lines

_____

_____

and that's more than I should say ☺

Be Blessed

ABOUT THE AUTHOR

Suba lives in the Evergreen State with his love and amazing children where he spends his time hiking, playing in the woods, gardening, hanging out with friends and family, and constantly giving thanks for the blessings in life.

www.ingramcontent.com/pod-product-compliance
Lightning Source LLC
Chambersburg PA
CBHW081455040426

42446CB00016B/3245